Beauty in Obscurity

Also by Andrew Drake and published by Ginninderra Press
Beauty in the Darkness
D&M Between 2 Men (with Martin Christmas)
Limerick Lovers (with Jill Wherry) (Picaro Poets)

Andrew Drake

Beauty in Obscurity

Thanks

This book is for the poems. When my poems are published, I view it as a celebration of life to each of them and a farewell. Thank you so much for visiting them.

I would also like to thank a few people for their endless support: Avalanche, Damien Brand, Sarah Brown, Jess Carr, Ryan Carr, Martin Christmas, Carolyn Cordon, Dyea Dolot, David Drake, Brenda Eldridge, Matthew Erdely, Michael Guarna, Samela Harris, Elizabeth Hutchinson, Stephen Matthews, Inez Morazzo, Alex Robertson, Tegan Sabine and Daniel Watson.

Beauty in Obscurity
ISBN 978 1 76109 547 4
Copyright © text Andrew Drake 2023
Cover image and author photo: Martin Christmas

First published 2023 by
GINNINDERRA PRESS
PO Box 3461 Port Adelaide 5015
www.ginninderrapress.com.au

Contents

The Journeyman	7
The Wolf and the Whale	8
Stronghold	10
Small Stories	11
Bread, Wine and Chicken Bones	13
When You Look My Way	15
Hidden Talents	16
Without you	17
Empty	18
Snowflake	19
Velvet Heart	21
Stop	22
In My Lane	23
To my Future Self	24
Cinderella	26
Mudskipper 2.0	28
Sixteen	29
I Hesitate	30
Ode to the Flamingo Shirt	32
Exit Stage Left	33
Thank You	34
Mistaken Lessons	35
Romance is Dying	37
Met Her For	38
The Antics of Semantics	39
Heartfelt	40
Love is to Love	41
How are you?	42
It Was a Warm Gesture	43
Sorry Love	44

Day-care	45
My Yesterday	48
What of the Spider?	49
Who Hurt You?	50
What Picture Did Your Eyes Last Take?	51
Getting Ripped	52
Pneumonia	53
Metamorphosis	55
How Can You Love Me?	56
My Heart Beats	58
In Retrospect	59
Gone	60
Teach Them	61
And I Love You	63
The Crayfish	64
A Living Crayfish	66
Acknowledgements	67
About the Author	68

The Journeyman

I wandered up to him that night. He stayed quiet.
His fingers intertwined behind his back.
His eyes held onto mine. He kept his ground.
This journeyman was heading nowhere,
so I stepped forward. He stayed silent.
He began to pace back and forth.
The journeyman lived day to day. The sun had fallen.
This wasn't a game for him. He was a fighter.
I saw no peace in him.

I took another step forward. He stayed wordless.
There were no more steps to take.
The journey was over. He kept his grip.
All expression had left his face.
No one had stood in front of him before.
They had all left, motivating him with their absence.
He seemed bulletproof. Nothing got in.
He could almost be anything.
I could almost be something.

He sat down in front of me. I stayed standing.
His fingers intertwined on his lap.
He saw an obstacle. He didn't owe me a journey.
I had no plans of leaving. He had no plans.
The sun was rising and he was ready.
There was no peace. He showed no fear.
He laid down and bled out at dawn. I stayed.
His fingers gradually parted. His eyes held on.
The journeyman never said a word.

The Wolf and the Whale

When a pack of wolves howl
or a pod of whales whistle,
I imagine they are singing
'This is where we belong.'
But what happens after
a wolf loses its pack?
Or when a whale wonders
why it wanders alone?

What if a wolf doesn't howl
or a whale cannot whistle?
What song would they sing
to finally belong?
Perhaps they both roam
because they were left behind
more than they were ever found.
Perhaps they are still searching.

I picture the wandering whale
calling out to the wandering wolf
'I know we are parted
by the land and the sea,
but I have met a thousand whales.
I have lost a thousand whales.
Do you believe there is a place
for us both to belong?'

And I dream that the wolf cries out
'Although you hold the ocean
and I hold the plains,
we both live under the same stars
and share the same sky.
We do not need to howl or whistle.
We just need to look up.
This is where we belong.'

Stronghold

You and I held onto our one-note
melody in a symphony of noise
longer than we held onto each other.

Our free verse fell in-between
harmony rarely matching the lyrics
while masquerading as poetry.

Admirers heard the rhythmic
chorus of our composition
and yet neglected our cadence.

We were set on repeat and played
self-conducted orchestras
that begged for a crescendo.

When listening to your outro
cascade silently from mine
I felt our music finish playing.

I still sing but now in a cappella
overtures because you taught me
there was a time I had a song.

Small Stories

It's Wednesday at 3.30 in the afternoon, which means I'm driving to you, thinking about how much I miss hearing your small stories. They were so big to me. You were so big to me, Dad. This was before your hugs became so brittle. Before hugging meant holding onto your ribcage, where more of you used to be, as you whittle away. You are less than half the man you used to be, physically, but still twice the man you see in me. I see you, but I can barely see you any more.

It's Wednesday at 3.45 in the afternoon, which means I'm hopping out of my car while working out what to say to you before I lose sight of you. But when I see what's left of you, my 'How are you?' turns into 'How much weight have you lost this week?', and my 'I love you' turns into 'Are you trying to die?', because I see less of you every time I see you and I don't understand why, so I waste time asking you about your weight while waiting for you to waste away. Instead of counting down your days, I'm counting down your kilograms and I'm not sure what the difference is any more.

It's Wednesday, after 4 o'clock in the afternoon, which means I'm trying to work out more ways to fatten you up while you refuse every idea I suggest, because apparently, according to you, attaching a sugar drip to your arm while you sleep is illegal. I threaten to hold your nose and pour weight gain drinks down your throat and you tell me to wait another kilo, but it's been 48 kilograms, there's less than 40 to go and you can't see that I'm losing you faster than you're losing weight.

It's Wednesday evening, it doesn't matter what the time is. I'm still missing hearing your small stories. I don't want our last conversation to be about your invisibility that you can't see and I don't want my memories to be filled with the image of you shrinking so drastically, while knowing that I couldn't save you. All I can think about is, by the time I begin driving to you next Wednesday at 3.30 in the afternoon, get out of my car at 3.45 and walk over to you, would have you disappeared completely by then? What story are you going to leave with me, Dad? Because you are brittle, but I'm about to break. But I guess this is the weight game, you lose it while I wait until I lose you.

Bread, Wine and Chicken Bones

We pull away from each other
the wishbone breaks
the silence
of our last supper.

The wish is never spoken of
so that it can't be broken, of
course to mean no matter what
it wasn't coming true.

So I never wished
or checked who won
in truth because we lost
each other
the moment we pulled away.

We were both lost
breaking up
the bone for nothing
but an empty promise.

We needed no wish
scattered bones
or false hope;
a last meal
for the condemned
nor silent wishful thinking.

We needed a voice
to speak and to listen
melodically and harmonically
to bring us closer.

We needed not to break or wish
but to mend and find
each other
as we broke bread
and drank wine
till we could justify
our loss for words

until there was nothing left
to say
or to save.

When You Look My Way

When you look my way, you see my personality. You see my sparkling eyes, supple lips and chiselled jawline, but you don't see my beard. You look right through my facial hair, my chin curtain, my trash stash, my mug with a rug.

When you look my way, you just see hair. You don't see the years that my beard stayed with me when everyone else left. You don't see the generations of bearded men that came before me. For I left the womb naked, but I always felt bearded. My first word was beard and I vividly remember sitting on Santa's lap while gazing up at his luscious beard, and when he asked me what I wanted for Christmas, I replied 'A beard.'

When you look my way, I want your eyes to fixate on my long, flowing facial hair while you whisper sweet nothings to it. I want you to love my beard and lather my beard in beard oil and comb it through my beard with a beard comb before running your beard balm covered fingers through my beard. I want you to sing lullabies to my beard while it's rugged up in a beard blanket that you knitted for it, and instead counting sheep, I want you to count each strand of face hair until it looks asleep, because beards can't actually fall asleep.

But mostly, when you look my way, I want my beard to become our beard, so when the world tries to get between us with their societies standards and their hygiene practices while holding their razors and their shavers, you and I will stand as one. We will face it with this bearded face and we will keep growing, together.

Hidden Talents

It's hard to breathe sometimes,
but easy to break down.
Anxiety holds me tighter
than anyone ever has.
It's tough to smile and laugh
constantly, publicly.
But it's easier than crumbling
into a mess.

Crying has become a hidden talent
because silence is contagious.
If I screamed any louder,
perhaps I'd make a noise
and you would hear me
before I completely
run out of breath
this time.

Alone.
But never quite alone.
Never quiet.
Never silent in my silence.
Never safe.
Never free.
Always trapped,
silently.

Without you

Without you feels like playing monopoly by myself. There's no one there to land on my mansion, but I still pay taxes. It leaves me with a hole inside of my heart, shape-shifting into abstract fiction created to fill the void of losing you. You are a hollowed tree of memories, overlooking purple carnations I killed because everything has been dying lately except for the constant reminders that you are gone.

Without you feels like leaving a souvenir shop empty-handed because your name is more than a word on a key chain that gets used when one door closes. I am Schrödinger's cat inside of the window that I was meant to escape through. The glass is smashed, while at the same time the window frame remains jammed. Both opened and closed; I am simultaneously free and trapped.

Without you feels like watching reruns of *Scooby-Doo*. In the end, I know who is under the mask, but I still hope an alternate ending will appear, where the ghost is real and comes back to life. It's impossible to switch off mysteries that I live for and you died with. We got so lost in thoughts of happy endings that we convinced ourselves that it was more than just a simple goodbye.

Without you feels like cancelling a reservation for two, booking a table for one and still sitting across from an empty seat. I am a prisoner, being force-fed sympathies to escape. My appetite for overthinking every moment we shared together leaves me filled up with loneliness while starving for ways to accept any kind of life without you. Through it all, you stay with me.

Empty

My car drives towards
paralleled destinations
while running on fumes.

Snowflake

I'm standing at the bottom of a hill in winter. I take a deep breath,
feeling the cool breeze fill my lungs, picturing myself as a snowflake
as it gently makes its descent onto the soft snow,
unaware of the tiny snowball that rolls toward it.

You used to be a snowflake too,
before being crushed by a multitude of you
that were once filled with empathy that mirrored me.
My snowflake fell victim in the collision course that was created not by you,
but by a thousand snowflakes before you.
We were doomed the moment winter began.
We were the momentum as the snowball grew.
We never had a chance.

I'm standing at the bottom of a hill in winter.
I breathe out visible clouds of frozen fear
as I see the mammoth snowball heading toward me.
I stretch out both my arms and both my legs,
knowing I don't have a snowball's chance.
Still, I stand my ground, and hope I can finally stop the snowball effect.

You never knew how to stop it when they started it
so you continued it.
It's easy to be cold when you're surrounded by it, so hit me again.
I will break every bone in my body
before I let this cycle pass on to the next snowflake.

Your impact leaves me so blue that I wonder if I'm breathing at all.

I'm lying at the bottom of a hill in spring.
I'm unable to breathe under a thousand snowflakes, evolving into a million drops of water
as I feel them melt into forgotten metaphors and lessons that were never learnt.
I picture myself as a single drop in the middle of the ocean.

You were never able to understand that just one droplet
is all it takes to create a ripple effect strong enough to change the tide.
For we were free the moment spring began. We were the momentum as the ripple grew. We have a chance.

I'm drowning at the bottom of a hill in summer. I breathe in water,
feeling the cool ocean fill my lungs
as the sun blares until millions of drops evaporate in the air,
gently making their ascent into the sky.

You were the last drop of water I choked on before I began to breathe again.
You used to be a snowflake…

I'm laying at the bottom of a hill in autumn. I'm picturing myself as oxygen.
I take a deep breath and breathe in hope.

Velvet Heart

I want to look into you
and feel the intensity
inside of your velvet heart.

I want to hold onto you
and feel the rhythm flow out
like our lives were erupting.

I want to circulate inside you
and feel the warmth you bring
flowing through your bloodstream.

I want to reside in your eyes
and feel the inferno ignite
every time you gaze my way.

Stop

It wasn't the trauma that fractured me,
it was the peace that followed.
Havoc birthed me
and gifted me a home in my ruins
to comfort my pain,
while peace gave me time
to overthink
and overanalyse,
over everything.

Peace was the burden that killed me
by showing me ghosts
that blamed and shamed
and trapped me,
because victims need wars
to be viewed as lessons
in fighting
and surviving
by never stopping;

Peace became my war
so that my future
would be the past
I could never let go of,
because wars need victors
and I could never stop
until I lost everything.

I can stop now ¶

In My Lane

I met you down the alley,
you were in my lane.
The ball was in your frame,
mine too and I could hear pins drop.
We didn't strike out and suddenly
you were all that stood with me.

We knew this was our chance
and I never wanted to split
but you were like a pin-up girl
and I felt like a pinhead.

We were the 7-10 and it hit me.
I wanted to pick you up,
you were my perfect 10
but I fell in the gutter.
I missed you the instant I knew
we couldn't be spared.

To my Future Self

It shouldn't have taken me
this long to write to you;
I hope that has changed.
I want to say sorry
for the way I blamed
who I am
and who I was.
Did you learn from us?

I currently believe
that I am where I am
to understand why I was hurt.
I'm learning that it hasn't helped.
Have you stopped hiding away
on your birthdays?

I don't even know if you will read this
because I don't know who I will be.
There were so many years
I didn't even think
you would exist,
and I just want to
keep apologising
for not believing in you more.

I hope you've forgiven me
for always expecting
too much from me.
Have you figured out
who you are
instead of believing
you were a mixture of
trauma and accomplishments?

I hope you've learnt
to drink more water
without needing to be reminded.
Also, not everyone hates you;
they wouldn't be reminding you
to drink water if they did.

I love you;
I never stopped loving
the possibility of you
even when I couldn't love me,
and although I won't be reading it,
please don't be afraid to write back
because there is still
so much I can't say
that I hope one day
you can.

Cinderella

You are Cinderella at midnight
running away from your happily ever after
and into the fictional words
that you desperately want to believe in;
too busy running out of time
to ever wonder why your glass
slipper hasn't vanished.

You are Cinderella the princess
wearing the outfit of a maid,
feeling like the third wheel of a unicycle
while questioning how he could notice
what he never knew he needed
until you rolled up
and then disappeared.

You are Cinderella in real life,
having conversations with animals
that don't speak
but they also don't judge you;
they notice you and appreciate you
even when you're wearing rags,
because they see the real you.

You are Cinderella at 12 a.m. on Tuesday
without a fairy godmother
offering temporary wishes.
You're in your sweatpants
running away in sneakers
from a prince who lines up suitresses
while masquerading in a ball.

You are Cinderella to me,
but I'm no prince charming.
My castle is as suburban as it gets,
I don't own a suit and jacket
and when I talk to animals
it becomes a two way conversation
that always leads to you.

So the moment I saw you
running out of the ball,
with no music playing
or masks charading,
I knew I would ask to dance
in this modern-day fairy tale
with my Cinderella at midnight.

Mudskipper 2.0

I bought six goldfish;
five died within weeks.

It must feel lonely
being the last goldfish,
forgetting everything
but their existence.

I gave away one goldfish;
it's lived for years.

I couldn't take care of it,
or swim or forget
how lonely it is to know
my goldfish outlived
so many loved ones
in spite of me.

I feel a little less alone;
you're still swimming.

Sixteen

I was 16 when he was conceived. Nine months later I remember watching the contractions on the monitor rise, as if it were a video game, breaking high score after high score; unaware of its meaning. It took 19 hours and when he was finally born, I remember singing. I conceal my emotions well, but that's my tell that I'm happy. I sang all night.

I never understood why people congratulated me for not leaving. I wondered if a father abandoning their child was so common that we had to celebrate the ones who would remain. My mum had left me before I had turned one; my dad had stayed. I'm no hero, just a dad who would sing bedtime songs each night because I couldn't help but sing when he was with me. He was growing up while I was still growing up, and as he grew, he would say to me, 'Remember to smile.' He saw me, especially when I found it hard to sing certain songs.

Some of my favourite memories are of him and I playing video games together, breaking high score after high score. He's beginning to break my high scores now and I love that. He's nearly 16 now. The moment I began to wonder if he was getting too old for me to sing him bedtime songs was the night he began singing them with me. I'm pretty sure singing is his tell too. Currently his favourite song to sing is 'Africa' by Toto, and each night we sing together, remembering to smile.

I Hesitate

You weren't normal for me. My ordinary days dream of a dark room, because stepping out makes me anxious of the nightmares that await, but don't really await. See, I hesitate in what to eat, so I end up not eating. I hesitate, in crossing the road, so I end up walking in circles until I don't have to. I hesitate in saying the right things, so I always end up saying the wrong things. And I hesitate answering the phone, so I leave my phone on silent and never pick up. But when you stumbled into me, I had no moment to hesitate.

You were the serenity to my anxiety. I began eating with you, and even when we didn't eat, you made me feel full. When I couldn't cross the road, you held my hand and brought me there with you. When I said the wrong things, and I always said the wrong things, you made me feel like they were right. And when I saw you call, I always answered. I stopped dreaming of dark rooms.

You never hesitated to hold me, while my arms couldn't decide how to hold you back; was I holding you back? You never hesitated to love me, while I couldn't find the right words. I could never find the right words! But you never hesitated. I should have known you wouldn't hesitate to leave me.

I wanted you to stay as you left, but you weren't holding my hand when you walked across the road so I was stuck. I just wanted to say the right things, I wanted to say anything to bring you back, but I couldn't breathe while anxiety swallowed my words, because no words could do justice, so instead, I slowly watched your silhouette disappear, silently. I turned the volume of my phone all the way up and I waited, but you never called.

Nothing was normal for me. I stopped dreaming of that dark room the moment I began living in it and I couldn't tell you the last time I ate, but I call you now, every day as I walk around in circles. The phone just never rings.

Ode to the Flamingo Shirt

I never knew when I first wore you
that I would wear you out.
Now ripped, like a baby
from their mothers arms,
I am left feeling ripped apart.

You were threaded for me;
Buttoned by me.
You were 100% cotton
and I was 100% certain
that you would always have my back.

They say the clothes maketh the man,
you made me want to be the man
you always saw in me;
the type of man that would give
the shirt off their back,
unless you were the shirt
I had chosen that day,
because I would never give you up.

However, you are gone forever now
and my love for you fills me with hurt.
I know each day, I will miss you,
my beautiful flamingo shirt.

Exit Stage Left

It's easy to laugh with an audience;
easier to yell with a crowd
because it's careful.
I'm unable to because I know
wars have started over less.

We are taught individuality
from people that view
a lifetime as a life sentence
rather than accepting
that the best moments
are one's that can't be exploited.

I know my curtain has called.
It's my time to exit stage left
but the show must go on,
so let them watch an empty stage.
Let them boo and build
a story that outlasts me.

Thank You

I am ready to run and wave
and say hello to people
walking down each street
while thanking every kindness
that surrounds my loneliness
with love and hope.

Mistaken Lessons

When she told me 'You're afraid of commitment,' I thought about my past because we don't learn through our successes, but by our failures and I've learnt a hell of a lot about love.

The first time a girl asked me out I was 13 years old. Before that, every time a girl looked my way, I hid behind a book. Two days later she asked me if I loved her and without hesitation, I said yes. She promptly dumped me, the amazing safety net in her balancing act. Moments later she asked another boy out in front of me. I mistakenly learnt that I was second best when I should have learnt that she didn't deserve my love.

When I was 15, I saw this beautiful girl and so I shyly, nervously whispered, 'You are beautiful,' and for that she called me a liar. After this I stopped saying it. I began telling girls how smart, kind and hilarious they are, but I rarely said beautiful because I was afraid that I wouldn't be believed. I mistakenly learnt to be silent when I should have learnt to tell her over and over again, 'You are beautiful' until she believed it.

At 17, I mistakenly learnt that I wasn't special when I should have learnt that she just couldn't see it. At 21, I mistakenly learnt that she didn't love me enough, when I should have learnt that our understanding of love was just different. At 24, I mistakenly learnt to stop trying too hard, when I should have learnt to try harder. And at 27 until present, I mistakenly learnt not to trust and to be afraid and to this day I don't know what the real lesson is yet.

So when she told me 'You're afraid of commitment,' I replied 'You're right,' but what I wanted to say was 'No. I'm afraid of love because every time I've felt it, it's broken and shattered me, and you scare me the most, because I have never loved like this before.' However, I mistakenly learnt to let her go when I should have learnt to hold on tighter.

Romance is Dying

Is it romantic to say that I would lie face down, above your grave, fingers intertwined with the grass that grows above you, because I would rather imagine that I'm holding you between 6 feet of dirt than wishing upon stars that you would come back?

Is it romantic to say that I love your body of work and your body, but if you died in my arms, I would still love you while holding onto your beautiful corpse, because how could I ever let go of you?

Is it romantic to say that if you were cremated, I would scatter your ashes inside of a tornado so that I could feel you around me, surrounding me while I dance within your storm?

Is it romantic to say that I get so scared of losing you, that I create these scenarios where you're gone, because I could never tell you how much you mean to me until it's too late?

Is it romantic to never say I love you because I love you too much and I know that the only thing worse than not having you, is losing you?

Met Her For

The first time I met her, she told me she couldn't understand me. Apparently, I spoke in clichéd riddles that never quite added up, like a man who purchases a glass house; a terrible investment, then proceeds to throw stones at it.

I remember her sitting there like a couch potato in my gravy boat when she asked me to be clear. But how can I be as clear as day when it was 9.30 in the evening? I attempted to explain to her that around her, I have the heart of a lion, but I'm banned from the zoo.

It went silent so I told her there was an elephant in the room, but as she was the only other person in the room, this did not bode well. I explained that it would be music to my ears to set the record straight. She was the cat's meow; I let the cat out of the bag.

She became as busy as a bee in my bonnet. I tried to tell her that I was the early bird to her worm, the ignorance to her bliss, the rock to her hard place, the knot in her knickers, but she left. She was out of sight but still in my mind.

I should have known before I met her, when she told me she was anti-similes and analogies, and honestly, I don't know what I metaphor.

The Antics of Semantics

They call me a superhero,
so I spread out my arms
and tell myself that water
is just heavy, semi-solid air
I can fly and suffocate in.

I let the current drift down my throat
and swim down my lungs.
The oceans body
shows the villains reflection
drowning while I begin soaring.

They call me a supervillain,
the hero in me vanquishes
to prove that this time
I'm saving the world.

I fly over the horizon,
washing ashore
until they call me nothing;
till I become nothing.

Heartfelt

wanted

I

quite to

never lined tell

words up. you

my how

but I

felt

Love is to Love

I define myself by what I love
and am surrounded by
sights and sounds
that my heart adores.

This way, I never need to love myself;
I just love and know that
my heart is more full than heavy,

because love is not a thing
I carry inside that weighs me down.
Love is what carries me.

How are you?

Why don't we talk about these things? We laugh when our friends mention getting drunk before noon on a weekday, because it's easier to turn a blind eye, neglecting their cry for help, rather than asking them why.

Why don't we talk about these things? We sit in silence when our friends draw blood instead of pictures. We see scars from self harm from their wrist to their forearm, which should alarm us, but we say nothing.

Why don't we talk about these things? Conversations don't need to get awkward when the reply for 'how are you?' doesn't begin with 'good'. How did asking about the weather become more important than seeing whether someone is okay?

If you're feeling uncomfortable right now, it's because we don't talk about these things. But we talk after them. We talk after they drank themselves to death, ironically raising a glass for them. We talk after their scars became too deep. We talk after their 'I'm good' were found to be lies; disguised, because they felt like they couldn't say I'm hurting and I need someone.

Sadness is heavy; we can't carry it by ourselves. We shame people for seeking attention until they need medical attention because we don't talk about these things. But maybe it is time that we start. So tell me, honestly, how are you?

It Was a Warm Gesture

I decided to keep
the warm hoodie
you lent me
in autumn

that you urged
me to return
throughout
this winter

which felt cold
of you to ask
yet with kindness
come spring

I will graciously
lend you
this warm hoodie
for summer.

Sorry Love

To be loved is easy to hold on to
while to love is to let go.
I tried holding on after you let go
because I forgot how to fall.

I remember feeling hurt
when you told me you loved me,
because love was mainly stated
by those who had hurt me.

I never doubted your word;
I doubted the ramifications
and questioned love itself
because it refused to answer.

To love isn't easy for me
because love feels like an apology
reserved for when we hurt someone.
I'm sorry for hurting you.

Day-care

When my parents drop me off,
there's a good chance
I'm going to cry…
until they leave and then I'll be
completely fine straight after.

I like the order that comes
from building block towers
but I love the chaos
of knocking them down.

Playdough tastes better to me
than lunch sometimes
and I knew the spoon
wasn't an aeroplane,
but you nearly had me
with those plane noises.

I often dig because I can see
above my head
but not below my feet.
My sandcastles
never last that long anyway.

I want to drink from
my favourite coloured cup
because I know that the taste
of water depends solely
on the colour of the cup,
and I enjoy watching
you cook a feast
only for you hear me ask
for plain rice afterwards.

I will ask you to swing me higher,
but not that high,
but higher again,
while hoping you don't realise
I can swing myself.

I want to ride on the tricycle
that someone is currently on,
even though it's exactly the same
as the tricycle that no one is using,
and when I sit down
to listen to you read a story,
if a child is sitting in my proximity,
I will say that I can't see,
even if I can see perfectly.

I love giving you high fives
and singing songs
with all the actions
and telling you jokes
that make no sense
and asking you to watch me
do something that isn't
all that impressive,
and holding your hand
while I see the world
one speck at a time
as I grow with you,
until I grow up.

My Yesterday

You were always my yesterday
no matter how many days passed.
In the past, we were more authentic
than silence; I could hear my heart.

When I said goodbye to my yesterday
I wasn't ready to accept it yet.
In my heart, you became my today
and tomorrow became yesterday.

So I went back one more day
to the day before we met.
You were always my yesterday
and our tomorrow never came.

What of the Spider?

I wonder if a falling fly was ever saved
by the silk web of a spider,
or whether its agonising journey
was rescued by another's bad intentions.

I want to believe that sometimes,
the evil in this world creates good.
That there's purpose in the suffering,
where villains are no more than lessons
and heroes are no less than survivors.

Who Hurt You?

You used to believe...

I often wonder, who hurt you? Who hurt you so much that a thousand truths couldn't repair and conquer their lies; their life's mission until remission. I want to believe that you can see your beauty, reflecting from my eyes while you try to disguise it. I know it's hard to see when your eyes hold all the water in the world, but I would drink the whole ocean if it meant you wouldn't drown.

I want to know the moment that the hate you were receiving, stopped you from believing in you. I wish I could go back in time and find the bully that couldn't fully understand the ramifications of their words. If I saw them...
If I saw them I would hold them in my arms and say, who hurt you?

The truth is, we've all been hurt, and we've all hurt because it's easier to hide behind hate than stand for love. It is hard to be a victim but it's easy to stay one and we were all victims once. The hurt, hurt. They have been hurt for so long that it's all they know; nobody showed them how to heal. Wouldn't it be beautiful if, when I asked the bully who healed them, they would say you? Perhaps you would start seeing your beauty in their eyes too. Perhaps you will begin to believe again.

What Picture Did Your Eyes Last Take?

You drew better than I took photos.
The exhibition to your life
is in pictures I keep telling myself
I will burn.

You created temporary drawings
in a fleeting life
to illustrate that change is permanent
and yet your eyes will never change
or close now.

I can barely remember
what your eyes look like any more,
but I know that I miss them
because they captured me;
burning my world down
in a flash.

Getting Ripped

You are so fit
but it gets heavy
when you make me feel
like a lightweight.

I'm not trying to flex
or get carried away
but all I ever wanted
was to lift you up.

I'm running on a treadmill,
going nowhere fast
while you avoid me
the way you skip leg day.

I wish I was stronger
but this isn't working out
because I will never be
as good as Gym.

Pneumonia

When did we decide that falling
was a pleasant feeling?
Because I fell for you and it hurts
worse than pneumonia.
We say feelings like it's a good thing,
but I feel everything around you
and not everything feels good.
I feel hurt and confused.
I am terrified and I feel sick.
We say lovesick like a term of endearment,
but I'm sick of it.

I was falling and you caught me like pneumonia and then
    infected me with your love.
I want to find the cure but this sickness is spreading like a bug;
butterflies flying throughout my stomach.
These symptoms have my heart racing, cold sweats, nausea,
    insomnia.
The doctor asks 'Have you tried exercise?'
Well, I've tried walking the world away and all I've gotten is
    withdrawals
harder than from any medication
they could have offered.

I can't quit you.
I'm addicted to our time, our moments,
our little piece of heaven that isn't always so peaceful.
I can't lose you.
It would have been better to have never loved at all,
but I love you…so much.

I can't live without you.
I'm in recovery from falling for you,
and getting sick from you.
I'm delirious and the doctor begs me to stay.
I rehab from everything but you.
There is no cure this time.
The impact of the ground sounds sweeter
than the impact of this sickness,
but I can't stop feeling
so I don't stop falling
and now it won't stop hurting
us both.

Metamorphosis

I will never be
your natural selection
because I evolve.

How Can You Love Me?

Thank you,
for smiling for me
every time I couldn't.
Some days I wonder how
you never gave up on me;
you always saw the best in me
and on those dark days
when I couldn't see it,
you showed me that my best
was right in front of me.

Thank you,
for crying for me
every time I couldn't.
Some days I wonder how
you never gave up;
you always saw the best
and on those empty days
when I couldn't feel it,
you showed me that your best
could fall inside of me.

Thank you,
for believing in me
until I could believe in myself.
Some days I wonder how
you always gave so much;
you never saw the worst in me
and on those final days
when I could feel it,
you showed me that the best
would never be behind me.

Thank you.

My Heart Beats

If I had the words
I would have written this
a long time ago,
revealing to you
that my heart only races
when I'm thinking about you,
so ever since I first met you
my heart hasn't stopped racing.

If I had the chance
I would have told you
that I feel more
in your slightest touch
than I ever would with
anyone's everything,
because almost nothing
feels like everything
when I'm with you.

I still feel you so much,
but I found the words
and lost the chance
when I saw you leaving
and I couldn't bring myself
to write them down
until you were gone,
knowing that if I had you
I would have more than a poem.

In Retrospect

I'm not lost or lonely,
but I've lost and I'm alone.

I don't miss you;
I missed having the chance to.

Gone

I went to run to you
to push it down;
not you away
yet I ran from you
to let it out;
not let you go
and yet you're gone.

I tried to hold out
so I held on;
not onto me
because I had you
to help me breathe;
not suffocate
and yet you're done.

I went to disappear
to make it stop;
not make you stay
yet I've been seen
to start the end;
not on and off
and yet alone.

I tried to be free
so I alone;
not even me
because I have gone
to let the dark;
not lighten me
and yet I shone.

Teach Them

He was born crying naturally and then naturally over the years was taught to stop, leaving him only with secret sadness. Toxic masculinity through whispers of boys don't cry didn't teach him to be strong but to be silent.

She was born pristine and unblemished and was taught to keep it that way, like Snow White. Be beautiful, bite the apple and expect an unexpected kiss while you're asleep because boys will be boys who turn into men teaching boys, while she may not be believed, even if she isn't silent.

He was taught that he was the accumulation of all of his accomplishments and nothing more so he never quite felt like he accomplished enough, while she was taught that she was an accomplishment, a prize to be won and then owned or thrown away until she felt worthless.

He was taught that his life was like a roller coaster hidden inside a still pulse, smiling stoically to people who didn't know that sadness, real sadness looks almost like a smile from the outside. While she was taught that roller coasters were exciting, making her heart race through fear and danger and so she found a boy who put her in the most danger and believed it was love.

He was taught not to speak up. She was taught not to speak out and now she's an abuse survivor and he didn't survive. We are dying, men and women, from what we were taught when we were boys and girls. We are dying while newborns are screaming and living so don't teach him and her that he can't cry or that she is property.

Teach them respect and empathy, and that they don't need to live silently. Teach the boys and girls how to become men and women before they are another casualty because their future should not look like our present. So let's give them a future and teach them that they can be anything they want to be.

And I Love You

Every time I felt like I wasn't enough;
that my smallest achievements
were the most I would ever reach,
I would look to you and see
that you were so proud of me.

You were the greatest hype man.
You made me feel like I was incredible
no matter what and in every step
you were there cheering me on.

I began to believe in myself
because you never stopped
believing in me.

I know that I am enough now
because I was enough for you.

I miss you already.

The Crayfish

Dad was proud of stories
that made no sense;
a nonsensical conformist
living a chaotically normal life.
I wish I could write about crayfish
living out their fantasies
or dogs with suitcases
catching buses in New Zealand.

Dad imagined a mischief
without the memories
while his reality ran on
in his world of dreams.
In fact, he was a sweetheart
that spoke contradictions
like a mundane riddle
he believed was unsolved.

I wonder what morals were shared
between Dad and the crayfish
that stopped his bags from packing
to travel with the labradors.
I picture him waving goodbye
to each dog at the airport
before creating a tale
that wouldn't stop writing.

Dad was proud of stories
that made no sense;
he never understood
my normally chaotic life
and in truth, his only riddle
was the unseen memories
and rough unfinished dreams
that the crayfish swam between.

A Living Crayfish

By my dad, David Drake
16.7.52–8.9.22

A living failure is better
than a dead crayfish.
No one can feel as helpless
as the owner of a sick crayfish.
Even if a crayfish intends to loaf
he gets up in time to get an early start.

Sometimes a noble failure
serves the world as faithfully
as a distinguished crayfish.
Sometimes a noble crayfish
serves the world as faithfully
as a distinguished success.

A living crayfish is better
than a dead masterpiece.

Acknowledgements

'When you Look my Way' and 'Teach Them' (published as 'Life Lessons') was anthologised in *Fleurieu Flow: Friendly Street Poets Goolwa Anthology 1* (edited by John Malone & Margaret Clark), 2019.

'Romance is Dying' was anthologised in *alchemy: Friendly Street Poets 43* (edited by Veronica Cookson & Lindy Warrell), 2019.

'And I Love You' was anthologised in *The Crow* (edited by Brenda Eldridge), December 2022.

About the Author

Andrew Drake is an established written and spoken word poet from South Australia. He was the 2017 South Australian Poetry Slam Champion, and a five-time state finalist. Andrew has found success in countless competitions, including winning at the Adelaide Fringe Festival three times, and winning the Yankalilla Poetry Slam in 2019. He was the featured poet in Singapore; in Bali; and around Australia; and has also performed in the Sydney Opera House. Andrew has run poetry workshops in Australia and in Bali. In 2017, he co-wrote a chapbook with Jill Wherry called *Limerick Lovers*; in early 2019, his first full-length collection of poetry, *Beauty in the Darkness*, was published; and in September 2019, Andrew's second poetry book, *D&M Between 2 Men*, co-written by Martin Christmas, was released. All books have been published by Ginninderra Press. Andrew was the convenor for literacy at the Gawler Show during their inaugural literacy competition in 2021.

www.ingramcontent.com/pod-product-compliance
Lightning Source LLC
Chambersburg PA
CBHW071033080526
44587CB00015B/2599